EARTHDANCE

How Volcanoes, Earthquakes, Tidal Waves and Geysers Shake Our Restless Planet

By Cynthia Pratt Nicolson

Illustrated by Bill Slavin

Kids Can Press Ltd.

Toronto

Kids Can Press Ltd. acknowledges with appreciation the assistance of the Canada Council and the Ontario Arts Council in the production of this book.

Canadian Cataloguing in Publication Data

Nicolson, Cynthia Pratt
    Earthdance : how volcanoes, earthquakes, tidal waves and geysers shake our restless planet

Includes index.
ISBN 1-55074-155-1

1. Volcanoes — Juvenile literature. 2. Earthquakes — Juvenile literature. 3. Earth movements — Juvenile literature. 4. Geodynamics — Juvenile literature. 5. Creative activities and seat work — Juvenile literature. I. Slavin, Bill. II. Title.

QE521.3.N53   1994   j551.2   C94-931561-3

Kids Can Press Ltd.
29 Birch Avenue
Toronto, Ontario, Canada
M4V 1E2

Edited by Valerie Wyatt
Designed by Blair Kerrigan/Glyphics
Cover designed by Marie Bartholomew

Printed and bound in Hong Kong
94 0 9 8 7 6 5 4 3 2 1

*For Donald,
who loves to dance*

Acknowledgements

One of the best things about writing a book like this is the opportunity to ask scientists about their work — their enthusiastic curiosity is infectious. Two people at the Geological Survey of Canada have been especially helpful. I'd like to thank Catherine Hickson, "the volcano lady," for sharing her experience at Mount St. Helens, cheerfully answering question after question and checking my drafts for accuracy. Thanks also to Bob Turner for his generous advice and encouragement. The contributions of these two have been invaluable.

My thanks go to Rosemary Knight at the University of British Columbia, Paul Hoffman and Verena Tunnicliffe at the University of Victoria, and Garry Rogers and Dieter Weichert at the Pacific Geoscience Centre. Each of these scientists has helped in my attempts to understand complex processes and to explain them simply and clearly.

Many non-scientists have also made valuable contributions to this book. I'd like to thank Kae Kane, Andrea McKay and my mother, Bernice Pratt, for their help. Thanks also to Blair Kerrigan, Bill Slavin, Lori Burwash and all the people at Kids Can. My editor, Val Wyatt, has kept me on track through this first book with her amazing ability to be both demanding and kind. I'd like to thank my children, Ian and Vanessa, for kid-testing activities and portions of the text, and my older daughter, Sara, for taking charge when I was busy writing. Finally, thanks to my husband, Donald, for his constant support.

Table of Contents

EARTH'S RESTLESS DANCE

Imagine a volcano popping up in your backyard. Impossible, you say? A Mexican boy named Cresencio Pulido might have agreed — until he saw it happen.

One morning in 1943, Cresencio was tending the sheep while his father ploughed their cornfield nearby.

Suddenly, a bowl-shaped spot in the field started grumbling. As Cresencio raced to tell his father, the bowl cracked open and white smoke puffed out.

The boy and his father ran from the field. Behind them, a loud hissing filled the air and fiery lava shot into the sky. The ground trembled beneath their feet.

That night, the Pulidos and their neighbours in the town of Paricutin heard thundering explosions coming from the direction of the cornfield.

The next morning, they found a baby volcano in the field. But this baby grew faster than most babies do — by noon that day, its cone was as high as a ten-storey building.

In the days that followed, the volcano continued to erupt and grow. Lava flowed from its peak and covered Cresencio's home and many others. The town's church was buried right up to its steeple. Luckily, no one was hurt.

After ten weeks, the volcano was 335 m (1100 feet) high, and the people of Paricutin had given it a nickname — El Monstruo. Cresencio's cornfield had turned into a rock-spitting, fire-breathing monster!

What's Going On?

Why do volcanoes spit fiery lava into the sky? How can an earthquake shake solid ground? If you've ever wondered about these things, you're not alone. For centuries, people have been shocked and puzzled by nature's tantrums.

In this book you'll find out why earthquakes and volcanoes happen. You'll read about people who fought lava with fire-hoses, a girl whose house split down the middle and a whole town that suddenly disappeared. You'll even learn how to make a mini-volcano in your kitchen and cook up some yummy lava rock. To find out more about our rambunctious planet, read on!

The Inside Story

Suppose you could take an imaginary elevator to the centre of the Earth. What would you find? Hop on board and see for yourself.

Tap a hard-boiled egg gently on a table — just hard enough to crack the shell in a few places. Next, slice your egg in half lengthwise. Voilà! You've just created a mini-model of the Earth.

   In the same way that the egg has a shell, a white and a yolk, Earth has three main layers — the crust, mantle and core.

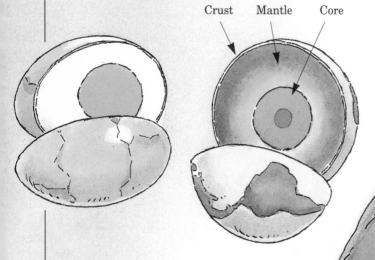

Crust   Mantle   Core

Unlike the egg yolk, Earth's core is actually made up of two parts — an outer core of liquid metals and a solid inner core.

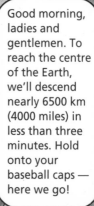

Good morning, ladies and gentlemen. To reach the centre of the Earth, we'll descend nearly 6500 km (4000 miles) in less than three minutes. Hold onto your baseball caps — here we go!

Ping!

We are now 3.3 km (2 miles) down, at the same depth as the world's deepest gold mines. The rocks around us are very warm — 49°C (120°F). Some warmth is left over from the fiery beginnings of Earth. More heat is produced by radioactive rocks, which give off energy in the form of heat. Going down!

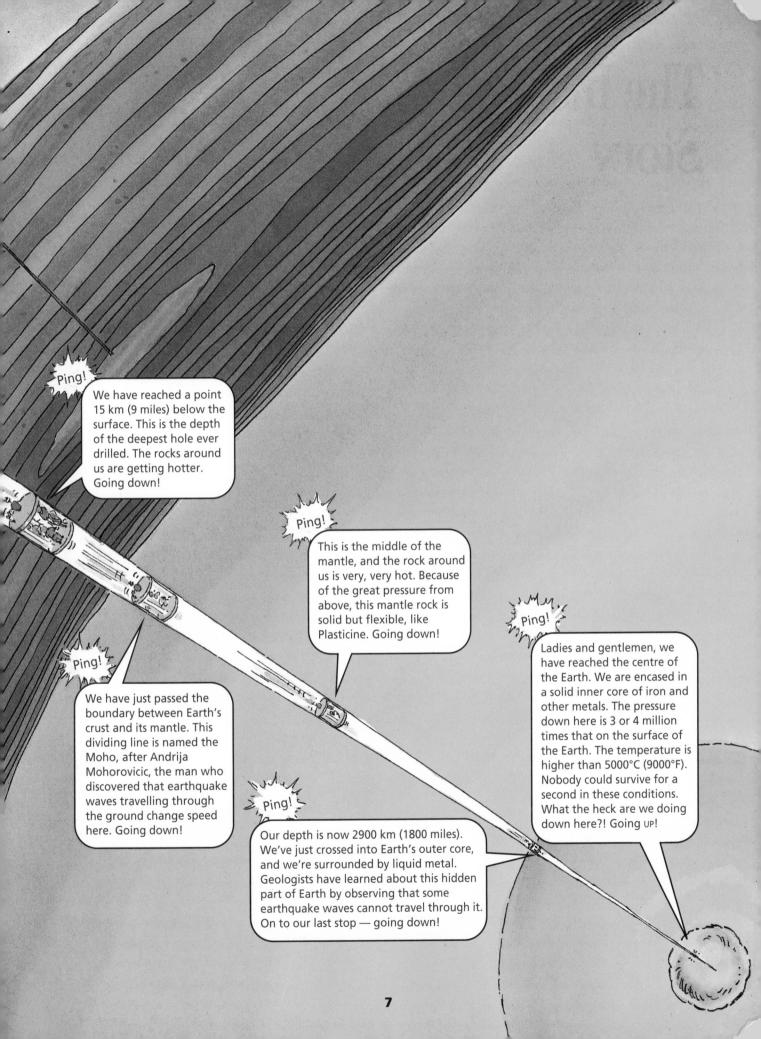

Steps in Earth's Dance

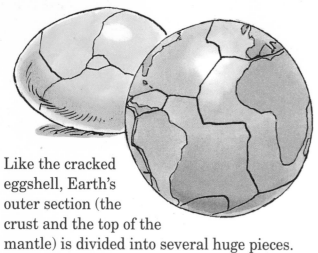

Like the cracked eggshell, Earth's outer section (the crust and the top of the mantle) is divided into several huge pieces. The edges of these pieces fit closely together.

Geologists (scientists who study Earth's crust and interior) call these pieces tectonic plates. Most plates are made up of both dry land and ocean floor. The jagged edges of two plates can meet anywhere: high in the mountains, along a coastline or deep beneath the sea.

Tectonic plates, unlike the pieces of cracked eggshell, are constantly moving. Like rafts, they float on the hotter, softer rock that is deep inside Earth. So, even though the ground under your feet seems to stay put, it's actually creeping across our planet's surface.

The plates move only as fast as your fingernails grow, but amazing things happen when they shift and collide in their slow-motion dance. Mountains rise. Oceans shrink. Earthquakes shudder. Volcanoes erupt!

Smashing Together

When one plate collides with another, it's like two cars hitting each other head-on. The plates bend and buckle, producing huge mountain chains.

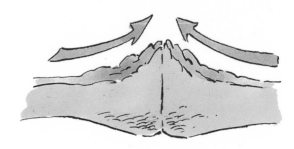

Diving Under

Sometimes the *sea-floor* section of one plate collides with the *land* section of another. Because sea-floor rock is denser, it dives under land rock. This process, called subduction, causes earthquakes and volcanoes.

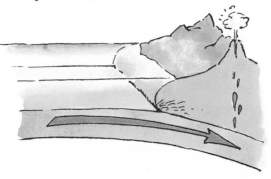

Grinding Past

At boundaries called transform faults, plates scrape past each other like cars being side-swiped in super-slow motion. If two plates get stuck while heading in opposite directions, energy builds up. Finally, the stress is too great. Rock breaks and the stored energy is suddenly released, creating an earthquake.

Gliding Over

Sometimes a plate glides over a "hot spot" in Earth's mantle layer. Heat rising from the spot melts the crust, producing chains of volcanoes or, in the ocean, chains of volcanic islands.

Drifting Apart

In some places, usually under the oceans, tectonic plates pull away from each other. Magma (melted rock from inside the Earth) squeezes into the split, adding new rock to the plates and forming huge undersea mountain chains. These mid-ocean ridges circle Earth like the seams on a baseball.

Why Are the Plates Moving?

Pour some grains of rice into a pot of boiling water. Does the rice move up, down and around? Geologists think that the hot rock in Earth's mantle moves in similar currents — dragging the plates across our planet's surface.

Other forces may also be at work. Magma squeezes up between two plates at a mid-ocean ridge. When the magma hardens and adds new rock to the plates, the ocean floor spreads outwards. But plates can't grow forever. At undersea trenches (the subduction zones near the edges of the oceans), plates sink back into the mantle, often producing earthquakes and volcanoes at Earth's surface.

Scientists believe that mantle currents and sea-floor spreading are two important forces in Earth's complicated and powerful dance.

The World's Biggest Puzzle

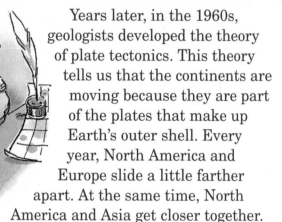

When map makers first charted the coast of Brazil in the 1600s, they were amazed at the way its dents and bulges matched the ins and outs of the west coast of Africa. No one could explain this jigsaw-puzzle fit until 1912. That's when a German scientist named Alfred Wegener published his theory of continental drift.

Wegener was sure that the continents were once part of a huge supercontinent, which he named Pangaea (Pan-gee-ah). He figured that when this supercontinent broke apart long ago, the continents drifted into the positions they're in today. But Wegener couldn't explain what caused the continents to waltz around on the surface of the Earth — this was long before scientists knew about tectonic plates. His idea seemed so far-fetched that other scientists called him crazy.

200 million years ago

Today

Years later, in the 1960s, geologists developed the theory of plate tectonics. This theory tells us that the continents are moving because they are part of the plates that make up Earth's outer shell. Every year, North America and Europe slide a little farther apart. At the same time, North America and Asia get closer together. How did scientists solve the mystery of jigsaw-puzzle coastlines? Here are some of the clues they used.

The black lines show the boundaries of Earth's main tectonic plates.

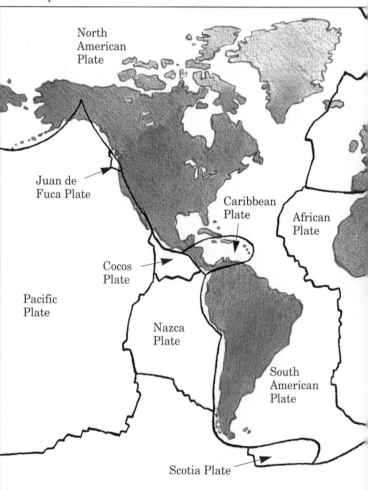

North American Plate

Juan de Fuca Plate

Caribbean Plate

African Plate

Cocos Plate

Pacific Plate

Nazca Plate

South American Plate

Scotia Plate

Fossil Facts

In Brazil and South Africa, archaeologists have found fossils of *Mesosaurus,* an ancient reptile with an alligator-like snout. But *Mesosaurus* couldn't swim the 4800 km (3000 miles) of ocean that separate these two places. Scientists think it's far more likely that South America and Africa were one large land mass when *Mesosaurus* was around.

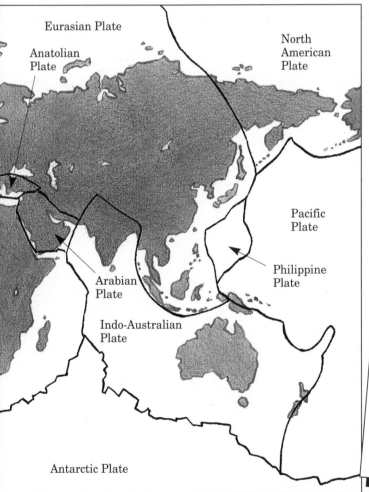

Matching Mountains

The Appalachian Mountains of the eastern United States are very similar to mountains in Scotland and Scandinavia. Rock formations in South Africa match those in Argentina. Why? Geologists believe that these lands were once linked together and that their mountains formed continuous chains.

Sea-floor Stripes

In the 1960s, while exploring the underwater mountain ridge that runs down the middle of the Atlantic Ocean, geologists made an amazing discovery. Rocks on both sides of the ridge produced the same magnetic patterns when tested. The matching patterns told geologists that rock is constantly forming at ocean ridges and spreading outwards as Earth's plates split apart. Wegener was right after all! Cruising continents have totally changed the face of our Earth.

Eurasian Plate

Anatolian Plate

North American Plate

Arabian Plate

Pacific Plate

Philippine Plate

Indo-Australian Plate

Antarctic Plate

See for Yourself

Place a piece of thin paper over a map of the world and trace the outlines of Africa and South America. Cut out these two shapes. Now try to place them side by side. Can you match up their coastlines?

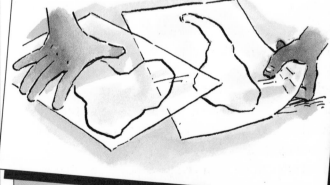

Travelling through Time

Imagine that you're an alien zooming in from another galaxy to orbit Earth. What do you see? That depends on when you arrive!

250 million years ago

You find a planet that has one huge ocean and one enormous continent. Peering through your spaceship's telescope, you spot small dinosaurs scurrying through forests of giant ferns.

65 million years ago

All the dinosaurs have disappeared! Peek through your high-power telescope and you see flowering trees and bumble-bees. The northern lands are still connected, but you can see separate continents in the south.

135 million years ago

You discover that Earth's land mass has broken into four main segments. Hovering near the evergreen treetops, your spaceship startles a family of long-necked dinosaurs and causes a flap among some of the world's first birds.

Today

You find a world with seven continents and three major oceans. Using your spacecraft's remote sensing equipment, you discover that the planet is inhabited by creatures who walk on two legs, wear clothes and talk with one another through holes in their heads. These beings look so weird that you decide to blast back to your own galaxy.

Bon voyage!

Unroll the Past

How far back can you remember? For most of us, even five years seem like a long time. But geologists measure time in millions of years. In this activity, you'll see time, from Pangaea to the present, rolling out before you.

You'll need:

- a pencil
- paper
- scissors
- glue
- a roll of toilet paper
- some small stones

1. Trace or photocopy the four stages of Earth shown on these pages. Cut them out.

2. Each sheet on your roll of toilet paper represents 1 million years. Glue the picture of Earth today on sheet number 1. (All of human history could be squeezed into the first 2 cm [3/4 inch] of this sheet.)

3. Now unroll your timeline and start counting. (Use small stones to keep it from blowing away.) At sheet number 65, attach the picture of Earth 65 million years ago. This is when dinosaurs and many other species suddenly became extinct.

4. Glue the picture of Earth 135 million years ago to sheet number 135. Pangaea was breaking up, but the dinosaurs were going strong.

5. Keep counting! When you finally reach sheet number 250, attach the picture of Earth 250 million years ago. At that time, all the continents were part of Pangaea.

6. Earth was formed about 4600 million years ago. If a roll of toilet paper has 300 sheets, how many rolls would you need for all of Earth's story? (Answer on page 47.)

VOLCANO!

Catherine Hickson loves volcanoes. In fact, she's made them her life's work. Catherine decided to become a vulcanologist (a scientist who studies volcanoes) soon after she was nearly killed by one.

The morning of May 18, 1980, was bright and sunny in Washington State. Catherine and her then husband, Paul, were camping near Mount St. Helens with their dogs, Crystal and Dawn. As she made her breakfast, Catherine noticed that the dogs seemed anxious and restless.

When she looked up, she got the surprise of her life. The whole north-east slope of Mount St. Helens was sliding downhill. The Hicksons stared in amazement as a cloud of steam and ash burst from the mountainside. The cloud grew bigger and bigger, billowing up and out towards them.

The campers realized they were in serious danger — a surge of hot gas and ash could quickly reach them.

As they sped in their car down the narrow logging road, Catherine looked through the rear window. The dark volcanic cloud rumbled closer. Weird bolts of blue lightning flashed through the cloud. A sound like the roar of a dozen jet planes filled the air. Lumps of mud and rock began to splatter on the windshield. Terrified elk bolted along the road.

DON'T LOOK. JUST DRIVE!!

Then the Hicksons realized that the road had looped back on itself. Instead of driving away from the blasting volcano, they were moving closer!

In desperation, they tried another route. But the main bridge had been washed out by a flood of mud and melted snow. Was there no way out of the volcano's path?

The Hicksons finally found a road that took them out of the danger zone. Three hours later, the couple and their two dogs reached safety. Catherine's frightening adventure had ended, but her fascination with volcanoes had just begun.

Before its eruption, Mount St. Helens sparkles in the sunlight.

Hot ash and gas explode skyward while a heavier cloud of rocks, ash and gas surges down the mountain's side.

The blast flattened tall trees like toothpicks.

Where to Find Volcanoes

Looking for a volcano? Most volcanic activity happens at the boundaries between tectonic plates. Here's where you are most likely to find an active, dormant (sleeping) or extinct volcano.

In a Subduction Zone

In these areas, one plate dives under another, producing magma. Pressure builds until the magma explodes out. Mount St. Helens is one of hundreds of volcanoes in a chain of subduction zones around the Pacific Ocean. The name of this sizzling circle? The Ring of Fire.

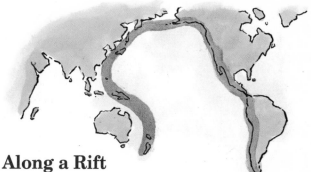

Along a Rift

Where plates move in opposite directions, magma spurts up through cracks in Earth's weakened crust. Iceland, a volcanic island, straddles the spreading rift between two plates in the middle of the Atlantic Ocean.

Over a Hot Spot

Some volcanoes are far from plate boundaries, at hot spots, where plumes of hot rock from the mantle burn through the crust. As the Pacific Plate drifted over such a hot spot, the Hawaiian Islands erupted from the ocean floor.

Discover more about these volcanoes on the following pages.

Mount St. Helens
A Subduction-Zone Volcano

Why did Mount St. Helens suddenly blow sky-high? Watch closely as the drama unfolds.

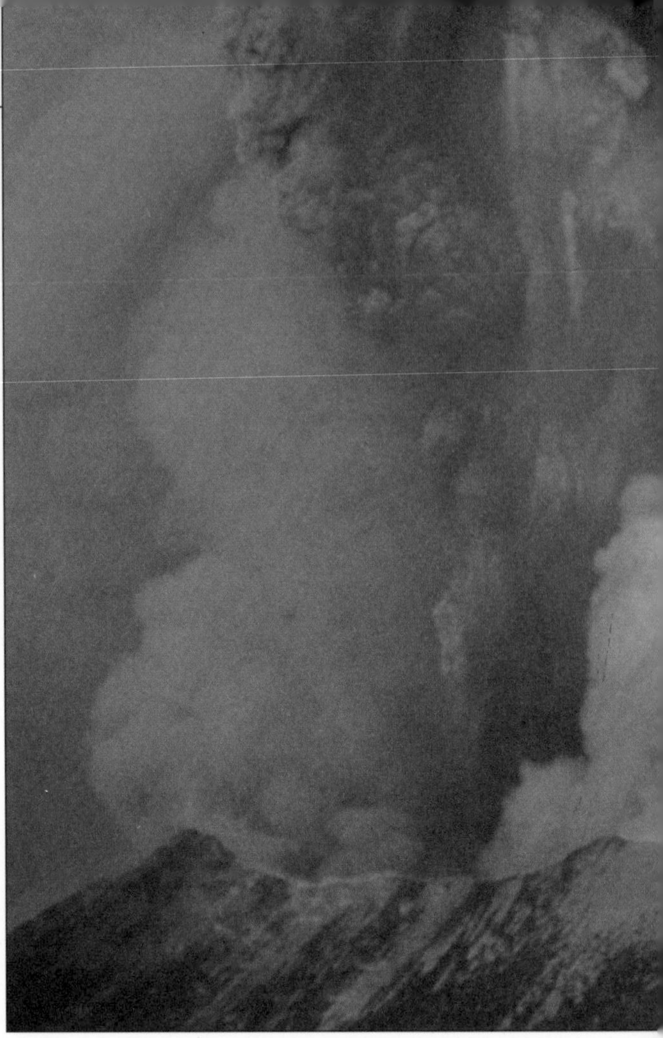

COUNTDOWN TO THE BIG BLAST

3...

Just off the coasts of Washington and Oregon, the small Juan de Fuca Plate dives under North America in a process that has been going on for millions of years. As it goes down, the diving plate releases water and gases into the rock above. With these additions, the rock melts at a lower temperature. Pockets of magma form. Because the magma is lighter than the surrounding rock, it rises upwards through cracks in the crust.

2...

Rising magma collects in an underground chamber. Some of this hot, gassy rock is pushed up through a large tube called a feeder pipe or chimney. But the top of the pipe is blocked and magma can't escape. Inside the mountain, pressure builds.

1...

In April 1980, scientists notice a growing bulge on the north slope of Mount St. Helens. Several small earthquakes and steam explosions had already shaken parts of the mountain. The magma is pushing to get out. What will happen next?

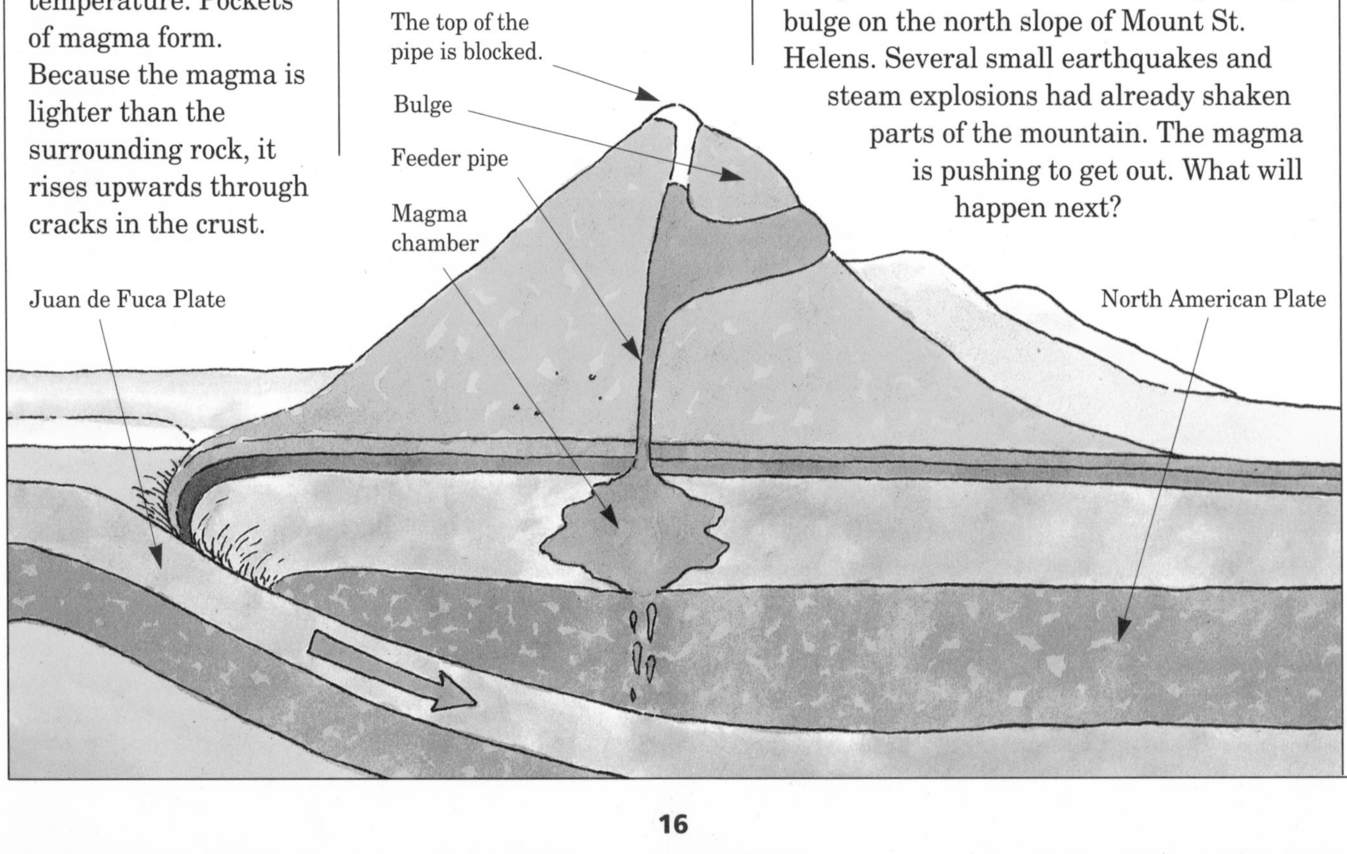

The top of the
pipe is blocked.

Bulge

Feeder pipe

Magma
chamber

Juan de Fuca Plate

North American Plate

BLAST OFF!

On the morning of May 18, the mountain roars its answer. A sudden landslide tears open the north-east slope. Pressure is released. Magma that was bottled up now explodes. Like a shaken pop can that's just been opened, the mountain spews out its contents. Ash and gases billow into the sky. Lightning zaps through burning clouds of steam and ash, which race downhill at 500 km (300 miles) per hour.

Everything in the path of this fiery avalanche is immediately destroyed. Thousands of large trees are knocked down and stripped bare. Homes and bridges are swept away when nearby river valleys flood with melted snow, mud and debris. Falling ash soon covers the countryside like a thick blanket of grey snow. In all, the mountain pours 4 km³ (1 cubic mile) of debris into the air. Within two weeks, its ash cloud has encircled Earth.

Magma Fizz

A sudden release of pressure after a huge land-slide triggered the explosion of Mount St. Helens. You can produce the same effect on a much smaller scale with a bottle of fizzy pop.

You'll need:

- a full plastic bottle of club soda with a screw top
- red food colouring
- a place outdoors where spills don't matter

1. Slowly open the bottle. The bubbles you see are carbon dioxide gas that's invisible when high pressure keeps it dissolved in the soda. By opening the bottle, you're releasing the pressure.

2. Add a few drops of red food colouring to the soda and tightly screw on the cap. Gently shake the bottle.

3. Pointing the bottle away from you, unscrew the cap. Stand back and watch your "magma" fizz out.

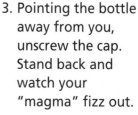

Under intense pressure, magma can hold large quantities of dissolved gas, mainly carbon dioxide. It's like a soft drink in a closed bottle or can. When the pressure decreases, as it did when the north slope of Mount St. Helens slid off, the magma can no longer hold all the gas in solution, and the mixture bubbles out. If the pressure has really built up, the bubbles can erupt with explosive force.

Iceland
Riding the Rift

Have you ever stood with one foot on a dock and the other on a boat that's floating away? Yikes! The whole country of Iceland is in a similar position. It's over a hot spot in Earth's mantle, right on top of the ridge between the North American and Eurasian plates. As the plates slowly pull apart, tension increases until — crack! — the earth fractures and a deep gap opens up. Steam and lava often spurt from the gashes in Iceland's fields and mountains, while earthquakes jiggle the ground.

TO THE RESCUE!

Brrrring! At two o'clock in the morning of August 23, 1973, a jangling telephone woke the mayor on the island of Heimaey, off the coast of Iceland. "There's a house on fire!" the caller exclaimed.

The mayor peered out his window and realized that this was no house fire — this was a volcanic eruption!

Just 13 km (8 miles) from town, the earth had split open. From a long gash in the ground, fiery lava spurted 150 m (500 feet) into the sky. Fine black ash blew towards the town, and a mass of rough, clinking lava crept closer and closer to the houses. Time to act — fast!

By eight o'clock that morning, most of Heimaey's people had reached safety on the mainland by braving the rough seas in small boats.

About 300 people remained, hoping to save the town. What could they do against a volcano? The lava was burning and burying the homes in its path. Even worse, it threatened to close off the town's precious harbour.

Then a scientist proposed a plan — spray the lava with cold water! If the melted rock cooled and hardened, perhaps it would stop the lava's flow.

Fire-hoses were quickly hooked up to pumps that filled them with water straight from the ocean. Crews aimed the sprays at the front edge of the lava.

As a crust formed, the volcano-fighters walked across it and sprayed more of the lava. It was dangerous work. Red-hot lava still bubbled under the hardened crust, and football-sized blobs of lava, called volcanic bombs, rained from the sky above their heads.

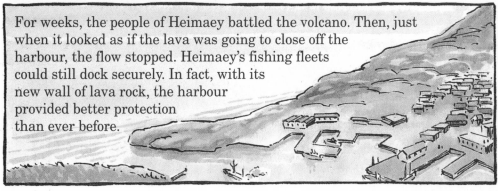

For weeks, the people of Heimaey battled the volcano. Then, just when it looked as if the lava was going to close off the harbour, the flow stopped. Heimaey's fishing fleets could still dock securely. In fact, with its new wall of lava rock, the harbour provided better protection than ever before.

Zap! Hiss! Kaboom!

Lightning flashed through a giant column of steam and ash as a brand-new island rose above the grey waves of the Atlantic Ocean. Just off the coast of Iceland, the small island of Surtsey first poked up its head in 1963 and continued to rise until 1967. Enormous explosions of steam accompanied Surtsey's arrival as magma from deep below the ocean floor met cold sea water.

Hawaii's Hot Spot

Have you ever had a fight with your brother or sister? Check out the family battle that rages in this Hawaiian legend about Pele, goddess of fire and volcanoes, and her sister, Namakaokahai, goddess of the sea.

Fire fountains shoot up from Hawaii's active volcanoes.

Go away!" screamed Namakaokahai at her sister Pele. Each goddess wanted to be more powerful than the other, and they often fought over who was stronger. But this fight was the worst yet. Both sisters raged and ranted until Pele gathered her family into outrigger canoes and set out to sea.

The volcano goddess sailed across the South Pacific for several weeks. Finally she decided to build her new home in the middle of the vast blue ocean. ROAR! Pele stamped her foot and plunged her magic stick, Pa'oa, into the sea floor. Lava spurted forth and the Hawaiian island of Kauai grew until it rose above the water.

For a time, Pele was happy. But Namakaokahai hadn't given up. Scowling with rage, the sea goddess attacked her sister's new home. Huge waves pounded Kauai's shores and flooded its lands. Steam hissed and rocks exploded as cold sea water met Pele's fires.

Once again, Pele moved on. Not far from Kauai, she plunged Pa'oa into the sea floor a second time. Another volcano burst forth and the island of Oahu was created. Pele and her family settled contently amid the island's lush green hills. But trouble was on the way.

"I'll get rid of you forever!" Namakaokahai shrieked as she lashed Oahu with ocean storms.

"No, you won't!" Pele answered, eyes flashing and hair flying in the wind. But once again, the sea doused Pele's fires and the volcano goddess was forced to move on.

One after the other, Pele created the Hawaiian islands of Lanai, Molokai and Maui. Each new home suited the volcano goddess and her family — until Namakaokahai appeared. When the sea goddess attacked Pele's home on Maui, the volcano goddess was nearly ready to give up. But she decided to try one more time.

South-east of Maui, Pele dashed Pa'oa into the sea floor and brought forth not one, but two new volcanoes, which formed the Big Island, Hawaii. "See, I'm just as strong as ever!" she bragged. Namakaokahai couldn't ignore the evidence. She took one look at the beautiful mountains of the Big Island and dove back to the depths of the ocean in defeat.

Pele stayed on the Big Island, where her lava still flows from the craters of Kilauea and Mauna Loa. To this day, Hawaiian people pay tribute to the volcano goddess and her fiery power.

Hawaii Today

The story of Pele is a powerful legend that was first told by the Polynesians, who arrived in Hawaii about 1300 years ago. It's also a surprisingly accurate description of the order in which the Hawaiian Islands were formed. These early settlers were good observers of nature, and they noticed how some of the islands had been worn down by centuries of weathering, while others were still covered with rough, jagged rock and active volcanoes.

Today, scientists explain the creation of the string of Hawaiian Islands by describing a hot spot — a plume of hot rock rising from Earth's mantle. As the Pacific Plate moves across this spot, the heat burns through, like a blowtorch piercing a sheet of metal. The hot spot stays in one place while the plate moves, so each new hole — and the volcanic island around it — is a little farther along the chain.

The Hawaiian Islands are part of an immense undersea ridge that includes 80 large volcanoes. To the south-east of the Big Island lies a new underwater peak, Loihi. Geologists believe Loihi may eventually rise above sea level and form a brand-new Hawaiian island.

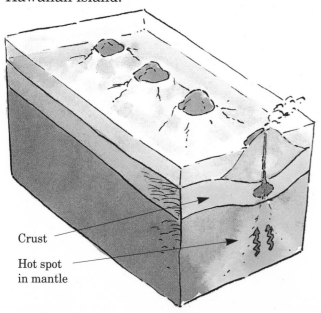

Crust

Hot spot in mantle

Poke a Plate

Magma piercing the Pacific Plate created the Hawaiian Islands. Here's how you can make a quick model of that long, slow process.

You'll need:
- scissors
- a plastic-foam meat tray
- aluminum foil
- a sharp pencil

1. Make a frame by cutting out the centre of the meat tray. Stretch foil across the frame and fold it securely around the sides.

2. Ask a friend to hold the pencil, point up, in one spot and to raise the pencil straight up each time you say an island's name. Now slowly move your foil plate from left to right above the pencil tip as you recite the names of the Hawaiian Islands — Kauai, Oahu, Lanai, Molokai, Maui and Hawaii.

The rising pencil point should pierce the foil, like magma pushing through Earth's crust. The holes you make are like the volcanoes that form this chain of islands.

What Comes Out?

Like an open-mouthed monster, a volcano dribbles lava, breathes hot gases and spits chunks of rock. Look out below!

Volcanic Bombs

Pieces of magma that cool and harden as they fall through the air are known as volcanic bombs. Bombs sometimes have spiral grooves on their sides that produce a loud whistle when air rushes past. Most volcanic bombs are egg-sized, but some can be bigger than a football.

Rough aa *lava (top) moves over* pahoehoe *lava (bottom).*

Lava

After magma has gushed from the ground, it is called lava. This molten, or melted, rock is extremely hot — between 800 and 1200°C (1500 to 2000°F). Even so, lava rarely injures people. It usually flows so slowly that a person could walk or run out of its way. The two types of lava flow have Hawaiian names. *Aa* (ah-ah) lava hardens into rough, sharp rock that is difficult to walk on. *Pahoehoe* (pa-hoy-hoy) lava hardens with a smooth, ropy crust. Walking over a cooled *pahoehoe* flow can be like walking on a sidewalk.

Volcanic Blocks

Sudden explosions sometimes break off large chunks of rock called volcanic blocks. A lava block can be as big as a house.

Dust and Ash

Volcanoes that explode with great force throw fine particles of dust and ash into the air. These particles are carried by the wind, and they often drift long distances. If enough particles are blown high enough, they may circle the world in an invisible cloud, causing long-term weather changes.

Glassy Lava

Bits of melted lava sometimes form glassy droplets or thin threads as they fly from a volcano. In Hawaii, the droplets are named Pele's tears, after the volcano goddess, Pele. And the thin threads? They're called Pele's hair.

Pumice

Lava that cools with lots of air bubbles trapped inside becomes pumice. Because it's filled with air, pumice rock is sometimes light enough to float. Sailors have even been known to hop on rafts of pumice for a truly rocky ride.

Lava Crunch

This candy looks and feels like bubble-filled pumice — but it melts in your mouth!

You'll need:
- a cake pan
- butter or margarine
- 25 mL (2 tablespoons) corn syrup
- 50 mL (1/4 cup) white sugar
- a thick metal saucepan
- 15 mL (1 tablespoon) baking soda
- a wooden spoon

Caution: Ask an adult to help you when you use the stove and always wear oven mitts.

1. Grease the cake pan with butter or margarine.

2. Combine the corn syrup and sugar in the saucepan. Cook over medium-low heat, stirring constantly, until the lava boils. Boil for seven minutes, stirring frequently. The mixture should stay light gold in colour.

3. Remove the saucepan from the heat and add the baking soda. Stir quickly until the lava is foamy. Use a wooden spoon to scoop your lava into the cake pan.

4. Do not touch the lava crunch until it is completely cool. Then break it into chunks and enjoy it!

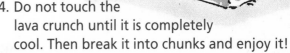

Volcano Portraits

If someone asked you to draw a volcano, would you sketch a cone-shaped mountain? Most of us would, but volcanoes come in many shapes and sizes. In fact, a volcano is any place where melted rock seeps, spurts, gushes or explodes through Earth's crust. Depending on the viscosity (stickiness) of its lava, a volcano can take any one of these three basic forms.

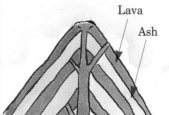
Lava

Ash

Composite Volcanoes

These volcanoes contain sticky lava that explodes with great force. Alternating layers of ash and lava, laid down in eruption after eruption, form a tall, steep-sided mountain like Mount St. Helens or Mount Vesuvius.

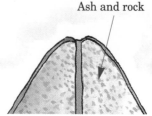
Ash and rock

Cinder Cones

These smaller, cone-shaped volcanoes are made of ash and loose bits of rock. Paricutin's 1943 volcano (see page 4) was a cinder cone.

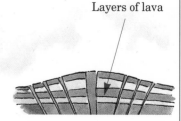
Layers of lava

Shield Volcanoes

These volcanoes are formed when runny lava flows over a wide area, producing a broad volcano that may have many side vents. Mauna Loa, in Hawaii, is a shield volcano.

Danger: Volcano at Work!

Slow-flowing lava rarely harms people, but explosive eruptions can be killers. Some volcanoes produce an avalanche of glowing rocks mixed with gases that flows down mountainsides at speeds of 100 km (60 miles) per hour or more. Vulcanologists call these avalanches

Molten lava flows down the cone of this Hawaiian volcano.

pyroclastic flows. (*Pyroclastic* means "fire broken.") Clouds of gas and ash blasted into the air can be even faster moving than the pyroclastic flows. They're called pyroclastic surges. The people of Pompeii and nearby Herculaneum were killed by pyroclastic surges from Mount Vesuvius. (For more about their story, see page 28.)

Mud flows, or lahars, are another danger. In 1985, the Ruiz volcano in Colombia, South America, threw out hot ash and rock that melted the snow and ice on its summit. The melt water combined with volcanic ash and produced a mixture similar to wet concrete. This river of mud flooded the city of Armero, which is 58 km (36 miles) away. About 22 000 people lost their lives in the torrent.

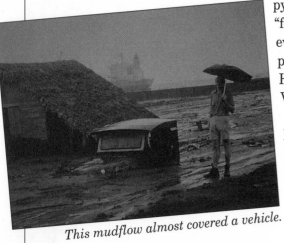
This mudflow almost covered a vehicle.

Volcanoes and the Weather

When volcanic explosions send gas and ash high into Earth's atmosphere, weather around the world can be changed. Close to the volcano, clouds of dust can darken the sky and block out sunlight, even in the middle of the day. Far away, airborne ash can cause temperatures to be lower than normal. Ash particles filter the light coming from the sun, creating some strangely colourful sunrises and sunsets.

The massive 1815 eruption of Mount Tambora, in Indonesia, led to the "year without a summer." In parts of the United States, snow fell and crops froze — in July.

When the Indonesian island of Krakatoa blew itself to bits in 1883, the explosion was heard all the way to Australia. Krakatoa's clouds of dust and gas floated around the world. In Europe, people were amazed to see a blue moon and a green sun.

Mount Pinatubo, in the Philippines, spewed ash and gas high into the atmosphere when it erupted in June 1991. By the end of July, Pinatubo's particles had encircled Earth. Scientists are making careful measurements to find out if chemicals in volcanic gas damage the ozone layer, which protects us from the sun's ultraviolet rays.

Make Your Own Volcano

This papier-mâché volcano can erupt again and again, just like the real thing.

Make the Mountain

You'll need:

- aluminum foil
- a small juice bottle
- water
- a measuring cup
- a bowl
- flour
- newspapers
- plain paper
- paints (water-based or acrylic)
- a paintbrush

1. Crunch a piece of aluminum foil around the juice bottle to form a cone-shaped volcano. Bend the edges of the foil into the neck of the bottle.

2. Pour 750 mL (3 cups) of water into the bowl. Add flour to the water a little at a time until the mixture is as thick as yogurt.

3. Tear the newspaper into strips about 5 cm x 15 cm (2 inches x 6 inches). Dip the strips into the flour paste and stick them onto the volcano cone.

4. Shape the strips into the neck of the bottle but don't block it. Cover your volcano with about four layers of newspaper, overlapping the strips in different directions. Let it dry for several days.

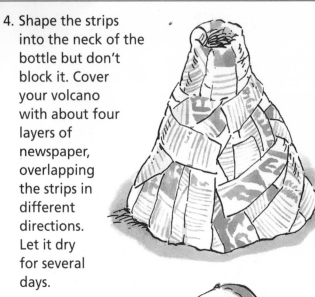

5. Cover the volcano with a layer of plain-paper strips dipped in a new batch of flour paste. (This will keep the newsprint from showing through when you paint the mountain.) Let this layer dry for one or two days.

6. Paint the mountain. If you're using water-based paint, cover it with clear lacquer when it's dry.

Cause an Eruption

You'll need:

- a large roasting pan or baking sheet with a raised edge
- a funnel
- 10 mL (2 teaspoons) baking powder
- a small bowl
- liquid dish soap
- red food colouring
- 125 mL (1/2 cup) vinegar

1. Place your papier-mâché mountain in the middle of the pan or baking sheet.

2. Use a funnel to pour the baking powder into the bottle.

3. In the small bowl, mix together a few drops of liquid dish soap, the food colouring and the vinegar. Stir gently.

4. Use the funnel to pour the vinegar mixture into the bottle.

5. Stand back and admire your mini-volcano.

6. After the eruption, rinse out the volcano and let it dry so it can be used again.

Can you think of several ways in which your model is different from a real volcano?

Pompeii

The Town That Disappeared

The people of the Roman town of Pompeii slept peacefully on the night of August 23, A.D. 79. That day, they had celebrated the feast of Vulcan, god of fire and furnaces. Some people had noticed a wisp of steam rising from nearby Mount Vesuvius, but no one was worried about the familiar landmark.

The next morning, Pompeii's residents were in for a deadly surprise . . .

Long after sunrise, the sky was still dark. Then grey ash began to fall on the town. Mount Vesuvius was erupting!

The ash downpour became heavier and heavier, clogging streets and collapsing roofs. Sulphuric gases from the volcano filled the air with a smell like rotten eggs. Chunks of rock rained down.

Some people protected their heads with pillows and ran from the town. Many fled in boats — they were the lucky ones. Other families hid in cellars under their houses or took time to collect their belongings. A little girl struggled to lead her horse to safety.

Suddenly, a surge of super-hot gas and ash blew through the city, instantly killing everyone in its path.

More ash buried the victims and their town. In one day, Pompeii, a thriving Roman community, had completely disappeared.

Pompeii Rediscovered

Almost 2000 years later, in 1860, the king of Italy asked an archaeologist named Guiseppe Fiorelli to direct the excavation of Pompeii. As the layers of hardened ash and pumice were dug out, Fiorelli's workers discovered odd-looking hollow places. These hollows were the exact shapes of the bodies of people and animals. Families were huddled together. A guard dog was trapped at its post. The little girl and her horse were caught trying to flee. The bodies had disintegrated, leaving only the victims' bones inside the hollows.

Fiorelli wanted to preserve these dramatic finds, so he invented a method of carefully opening a cavity and filling it with plaster. Now, instead of a hollow form, we can see a three-dimensional replica of the person who died. Fiorelli's method has also been used to make casts of furniture, trees and animals caught in the blast.

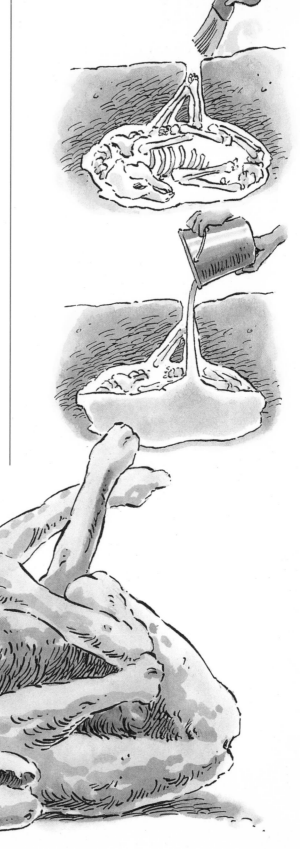

EARTH

It was a cold March evening in Anchorage, Alaska. Eight-year-old Anne Thomas was watching T.V. with her mother and her younger brother, David, in their home overlooking the ocean. Suddenly, they heard a distant rumbling. Anne and David were puzzled, but Mrs. Thomas had heard the sound before. "Earthquake!" she yelled.

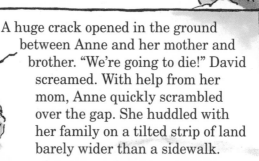

Without stopping to put on their shoes, Anne and her family dashed out into the snow. Then the jolting began. The Thomases were thrown to the ground, and Anne watched from a snowbank as their house was ripped apart. Terrible sounds of crashing glass and tearing wood filled the air. The entire hillside had collapsed and was sliding towards the sea.

A huge crack opened in the ground between Anne and her mother and brother. "We're going to die!" David screamed. With help from her mom, Anne quickly scrambled over the gap. She huddled with her family on a tilted strip of land barely wider than a sidewalk.

Before Anne could catch her breath, the little chunk of land plunged the Thomases downhill on a crazy roller-coaster ride. They landed at the bottom of the crumbling cliff.

For the next 15 minutes, Anne and her family scrambled over huge chunks of earth and snow. Anne made a brave effort to shinny up a tree trunk, but she could only climb a short distance before she slid back down. The top of the cliff was still no closer. Would this real-life nightmare never end?

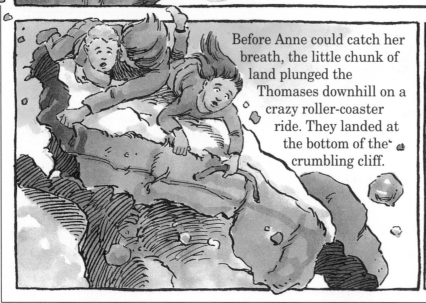

QUAKE!

Then, a miracle! The Thomases saw a man peering down at them from the edge of the cliff. They screamed and waved but he disappeared.

After what seemed like a very long time, the man returned with help. One of the rescuers climbed down the bank. He wrapped Anne in his jacket and picked up David. Together with Anne's mother, they made their way up the steep slope. People waiting at the top hauled them over the final rise. Safe at last!

Anne wore her rescuer's jacket for a week. It reminded her that she had been shaken by one of the world's worst earthquakes — and survived.

The Thomas home was one of many destroyed in the Anchorage earthquake.

The huge earthquake that hit the Alaska coast on March 27, 1964, toppled towns and triggered avalanches. It also caused a tsunami (tidal wave). Residents of Port Alberni, British Columbia, were shocked when 7 m (23 feet) of water flooded their town 4 1/2 hours after the quake. Later that day, the tsunami crashed into the shores of California and Hawaii. The earthquake's energy spread great distances through the ground as well. When its ripples reached Florida, on the other side of the continent, the land rose and fell 6 cm (2 1/2 inches).

Earthquake Power

Gigantic jolt — or gentle jiggle? Every day, more than a thousand earthquakes shake the surface of our planet. Most are weak tremors. If one struck, you might think a large truck had rumbled past. But each year, a few big quakes knock down buildings and cause landslides and floods. Tsunamis sometimes follow, bringing with them more destruction.

Though they're often called tidal waves, tsunamis have nothing to do with the tides. These monster waves travel across the ocean at speeds of up to 800 km (500 miles) per hour and can rise to heights of more than 20 m (65 feet). Most tsunamis occur in the Pacific Ocean, where they are set off by underwater tremors and eruptions in the Ring of Fire (see page 15).

When they crash into distant shores, tsunamis can cause horrendous destruction. Millions of sea turtles in Nicaragua were killed in 1992 when a large tsunami washed them from their breeding grounds. The gigantic eruption of the

Indonesian island volcano Krakatoa in 1883 was accompanied by earthquakes and huge waves that flooded surrounding islands and flattened many villages. At least 36 000 people were killed. The biggest tsunami on record hit the Ryukyu Islands near Japan in 1971. It was nearly as high as a nine-storey building.

A tsunami in Seward, Alaska, left a shambles of houses and boats.

Measuring the Shake

To tell how weak or strong an earthquake is, scientists use a seismograph. When a quake shakes the ground, a pen attached to a weight records a wiggly line on a moving strip of paper. The harder the ground shakes, the more the pen moves and the bigger the wiggles. The resulting paper record is called a seismogram.

In 1935, geologist Charles Richter invented a scale that gives each earthquake a rating (or magnitude) based on the height of its tallest seismogram wiggle. Each whole number on the Richter scale represents an earthquake 10 times stronger than those of a quake rated one level lower. For instance, an earthquake measuring 7.2 on the Richter scale shakes the ground 10 times more than one measuring 6.2 and 100 times more than a 5.2 quake. Can you figure out how many 4.0 quakes it takes to equal the vibration of one 7.0 quake? (Answer on page 47.)

Because the Richter scale isn't accurate past magnitude 7.5, seismologists now use other ways of measuring a quake's power. With the help of computers, they calculate the size of the fault and the distance rock slips. The largest earthquake ever measured this way shook Chile in 1960. Its magnitude? A whopping 9.5.

Seis-ing Things Up

Earthquake waves are called seismic waves. A scientist who studies earthquakes is a seismologist. Scientists measure earthquake waves on machines called seismometers. All of these words come from the Greek word *seismos*, which means "to shake."

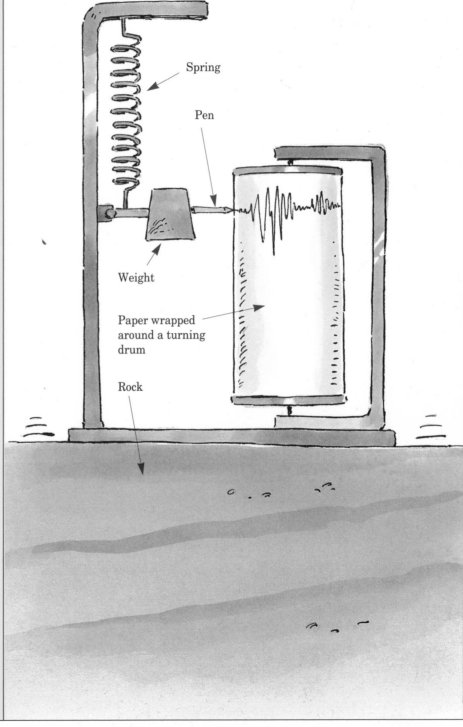

Spring

Pen

Weight

Paper wrapped around a turning drum

Rock

Quake Questions? Quick Answers!

Earthquakes are complicated. Seismologists have learned a lot about why and where quakes happen, but they're still stumped by one big question — when will a quake occur?

Why Do Earthquakes Happen?

The huge slabs, or tectonic plates, that form Earth's crust are constantly on the move.

Wherever two plates grind past each other, rock is squeezed, bent and stretched. Enormous stresses build up.

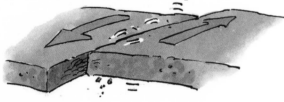

Eventually, rock breaks and the plates lurch into new positions. The sudden release of energy sends seismic (earthquake) waves rippling away from the breaking point in all directions.

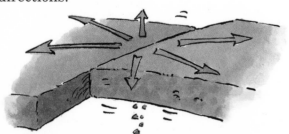

Create a Quake

To see how earthquakes happen, try this experiment.

You'll need:
- 2 pieces of sandpaper
- 2 blocks of wood
- a hammer and several small nails

1. Wrap sandpaper around each block of wood and attach it firmly using the hammer and nails.

2. Press the blocks together. Now try to slide one forward and the other back.

What happens? The bits of sand are like pieces of rock along the deep crack, or fault line, between two tectonic plates. They keep the blocks from sliding — until the force of your pushing becomes too strong. Then they jerk past each other. In earthquake areas, sudden movements of the plates release large amounts of energy, which create earthquakes.

Where Do Earthquakes Happen?

Earthquakes usually occur at the boundaries between tectonic plates. At some plate boundaries, or faults, like the one off the coast of Japan, an ocean plate dives under a lighter land plate. At other boundaries, plates collide head-on. That's what's happening  in northern India and Tibet, where smashing tectonic plates have created the Himalaya Mountains and caused many earthquakes.

Earthquakes also occur in rift zones, like East Africa, where two plates are pulling away from each other.

In some spots, two plates slide past each other, heading in different directions. For instance, the Pacific Plate is slipping north alongside the North American Plate at the San Andreas Fault in California. In 1906, the two sides of the fault shifted, and a devastating earthquake rocked San Francisco. One eye witness described it like this: "There was a deep rumble, deep and terrible, and then I could see it actually coming up Washington Street. The whole street was undulating. It was as if the waves of the ocean were coming towards me."

Another major earthquake shook San Francisco in 1989. Just as a World Series baseball game was about to begin, the announcer said "Oh my God. We're having an earthquake." The stadium was shaken, but everyone there was safe. Other parts of the city weren't so lucky. Some freeway sections collapsed, and older buildings on soft soil toppled over. But modern buildings and well-built bridges, such as the Golden Gate Bridge, stood up to the shaking.

Californians got another jolt when an earthquake shook the city of Los Angeles in January 1994. The 40-second quake killed 60 people and caused billions of dollars in damage to homes, buildings and freeways. Traffic was snarled for months as L.A. residents struggled to drive to work in their damaged city.

Because both volcanoes and earthquakes are caused by clashing tectonic plates, they're often found in the same places.

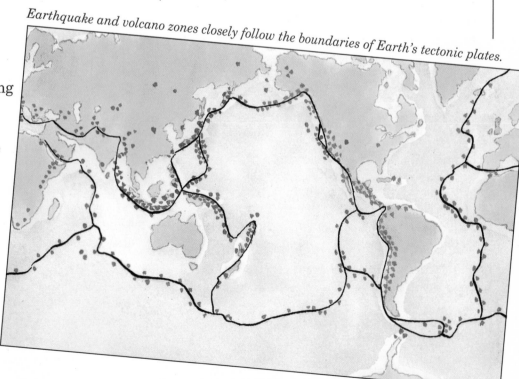

Earthquake and volcano zones closely follow the boundaries of Earth's tectonic plates.

How Do Earthquakes Begin?

Every earthquake begins at a focus, a point where rock that is under pressure first breaks and shifts position. This point can be up to 700 km (450 miles) below ground. From the focus, earthquake waves spread out in all directions: up, down and sideways. The place on Earth's surface directly above an earthquake's focus is called the epicentre.

Epicentre

Earthquake waves lose power as they move away from their starting point. In this experiment, you can see why most earthquake damage usually occurs at or near the epicentre.

You'll need:

- dominoes or thin rectangular blocks
- a cardboard box

1. Build a block or domino house on top of the box, near one side. Now build an identical house closer to the opposite side.

2. Tap the box top several times at a point near one of the houses. Which house falls down first?

How Do Earthquakes Spread?

Put your ear to one end of a wooden table. Ask a friend to tap lightly on the other end. What do you hear? In much the same way as sound waves travel through the table to your ear, seismic waves travel through the Earth.

Some seismic waves, called surface waves, move along the top of the ground. These waves can cause great damage when they hit towns and cities. Other waves, called primary and secondary body waves, speed through Earth's inner layers. Primary waves (P-waves) travel faster than secondary waves (S-waves) and can ripple right through the planet's liquid outer core. A P-wave takes about 20 minutes to travel from one side of the Earth to the other. S-waves are slower and can only move through solid rock. By comparing the travelling times and paths of P-waves and S-waves, scientists have learned a lot about the inside of the Earth.

To see how the two types of body waves travel, grab a Slinky toy and a skipping rope.

1. Stretch the Slinky out on the floor. Ask a friend to hold the other end. Quickly push and pull the Slinky. Can you see the ripple that travels through the Slinky as the wave energy moves from one end to the other? A P-wave travels through the ground in much the same way. Seismic energy scrunches and stretches rocks, just as your motion compressed and expanded the coils in the Slinky.

2. Now ask a friend to hold one end of a skipping rope while you shake the other end up and down. The high and low points along your skipping rope are like the troughs and peaks of an S-wave. Can you see how an S-wave travels differently from the P-wave you made with the Slinky?

3. Try building different sorts of houses and tapping in different places.

Your tapping makes vibrations in the box that are just like earthquake tremors in the ground. In both cases, buildings close to the source of the shaking usually feel its effects the most.

Strong and Flexible

Most earthquake injuries are caused by falling debris and collapsing buildings. In parts of the world where houses are made of loose stones or bricks, even a medium-sized earthquake can hurt a lot of people. To prevent the kind of destruction shown in the photos below, modern buildings have been designed to withstand earthquakes. A well-built house with a wood frame and concrete base will usually remain intact. Even tall office buildings are earthquake-resistant when they are constructed with steel frames that can bend without breaking during a quake.

Top: Collapsing buildings in the 1906 San Francisco earthquake caused injuries and deaths. Bottom: While modern buildings may move, new construction methods keep them from collapsing.

"A strong earthquake will probably

Seismologists usually can't predict when an earthquake will happen. In rare cases, however, a successful warning has been given. The residents of Haicheng, China, were alerted five hours before an earthquake hit their area. How? By a series of strange events . . .

On a cold afternoon in January 1975, a group of children was skating happily on a pond in Haicheng, China. Suddenly they saw frogs jumping up through holes in the ice.

As the children hurried home to tell their families, they discovered two frozen snakes lying on top of the snow. One boy grabbed a stiff snake — this would scare his little sister!

The children's story about what they had seen at the skating pond wasn't the only strange tale told that winter in Haicheng.

People noticed pets acting oddly. Dogs that usually were quiet barked wildly. Calm, gentle cats howled all night. Ducks and chickens cackled and flapped in their pens.

Other animals seemed to be upset as well. Rats came out of their hiding places and scurried through the streets.

At the zoo, tigers and lions anxiously padded back and forth in their cages. A deer tried to leap a fence and broke its leg. A panda rocked from side to side, holding its head in its paws and moaning loudly.

All of these strange things were reported to the earthquake experts. They also heard that warm water had bubbled up through cracks in a frozen pond and that wells had filled with foamy, stinking liquid.

occur tonight"

They could see for themselves how the sky glowed orange at night. And they could hear the ominous booming sounds.

The experts had already noted many small tremors in the area. Then, on February 4, they decided that a major earthquake was about to happen. At dinner time the next evening, they announced, "A strong earthquake will probably occur tonight. We insist that all people leave their homes and animals leave their stables."

To keep people outdoors, movies were shown in the public square.

Just as the first film ended, a flash of lightning brightened the sky. Thunder roared and the earth shook like a stormy sea.

Haicheng was hit by an earthquake measuring 7.3 on the Richter scale. Most of its loosely built houses collapsed. Thirty people who ignored the warnings died. But for the first time ever, a big earthquake had been accurately predicted. The children from the skating pond, and most of Haicheng's other residents, had been saved.

After the successful Haicheng prediction, seismologists around the world hoped they could start forecasting earthquakes accurately. That turned out to be much harder than many expected. Each quake is different and most give no clear warning signals. Today, geologists study tiny cracks in rocks, underground water levels, animal behaviour and the history of earthquakes in a certain area. One day they may be able to answer the question, When will the next earthquake happen?

MOUNTAINS, HOT VENTS, GEYSERS AND MORE

In the fall of 1835, the British ship *Beagle* sailed into the port of Valparaiso, Chile. From its deck, 25-year-old Charles Darwin stared eagerly at the mountainous shoreline before him. Here at last!

The young English scientist was intensely curious about the wild and beautiful land he had voyaged halfway around the world to see.

Darwin set off to explore the Andes Mountains. He chipped away at rocks, collected fragments to take home and kept notes in his journal.

High in the Andes, Darwin made a puzzling discovery: layers of rock filled with fossils of seashells. What were the remains of sea creatures doing on a mountain peak?

Most people thought Earth was only a few thousand years old. They believed its land-forms hadn't changed much during that time. Darwin didn't agree. He reasoned that the seashells must have been lifted from the ocean floor — a process that would have taken millions of years. Darwin wrote, "Nothing, not even the wind that blows, is so unstable as the level of the crust of the earth."

Charles Darwin later became famous for his theory of how plants and animals evolved on Earth. But he was always stumped by the puzzle of the fossil seashells. What mighty force could raise mountains from ancient sea floors?

We now know that the Andes Mountains of South America have been pushed up by the collision of two tectonic plates. The Nazca Plate, a huge slab of Pacific Ocean floor, is sliding into South America. Because it is denser, the sea-floor plate thrusts under the land, crumpling the edge of the continent. The Andes Mountains are like enormous wrinkles of rock rising towards the sky.

Mountain Making

Geologists divide mountains into three main types.

Fold Mountains

All of the world's great mountain ranges, including the Andes, Rockies, Alps and Himalayas, have been wrinkled up (or folded) during the crashing together of two tectonic plates.

Block Fault Mountains

Some mountains, like those in the Great Rift Valley of East Africa and the Sierra Nevada of California, rise when blocks of land slip up or down along fault lines in Earth's crust.

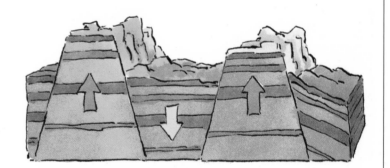

Volcanic Mountains

Repeated eruptions can produce large individual mountains, such as Mauna Loa in Hawaii. Volcanic mountains also form on top of fold-mountain ranges.

Wrinkle Some Mountains

To see what happens when tectonic plates collide, all you need is a hand towel. Press one hand flat on each end of the towel and slowly bring your hands together. The buckling and bending you see is a small-scale version of the same process that has created awe-inspiring mountain chains around the world.

Hot Vents

Journey to the Bottom of the Sea

When a team of scientists set out in 1977 to explore the hidden world on the bottom of the ocean, they expected to discover rocks and minerals — not living creatures that looked like something from outer space.

Off the north-west coast of South America, the team lowered a thermometer and special remote-controlled camera into the ocean.

When the equipment was pulled up again, the scientists discovered that there were warm spots at the bottom of the cold ocean. Pictures showed smooth, pillowy lava rocks and something unexpected — giant clams.

How could the clams survive where there was no light and little food? Were there other creatures down there in the darkness? The scientists had to see for themselves.

In the mini-submarine *Alvin*, three scientists journeyed 2.5 km (1½ miles) down to the ocean floor.

Alvin's searchlight pierced the milky blue water, illuminating hundreds of clams clinging to the black rocks. The clams were the size of small watermelons.

The scientists had found a hot vent — a geyser of warm water and minerals erupting from the ocean floor. Hot vents occur where the sea floor spreads between two tectonic plates. At some spots, sea water sinks into cracks in the sea floor, where it's heated by underground magma and saturated with minerals. Under intense pressure, this hot water spurts back out into the ocean. In the cold, dark world at the bottom of the ocean, a hot vent can be like an oasis in the desert.

After their first discovery, the scientists found other hot vents, each with its own animal community. Some of the animals they discovered were so new they didn't even have names. Based on what the animals looked like, the scientists gave them nicknames, like "Dandelion" and "Spaghetti."

One hot-vent site, which the scientists called the Garden of Eden, was dominated by huge tube worms. Clustered around the vent, the red-tipped worms poked from their white cases like giant tubes of lipstick. Carpets of bacteria coated the pillowy rocks around them. In the same way that green plants grow on the energy from sunshine, these bacteria thrive on the energy of hot-vent minerals. And, just as you eat plants like lettuce and potatoes, other hot-vent creatures eat the bacteria. But the tube worms can't eat — they don't have any mouths or stomachs! Instead, they feed directly on special bacteria that grow right inside their bodies.

Since 1977, hot-vent communities have been found in many undersea spots around the world. Scientists are fascinated by the unusual animals living in these hidden habitats. Some even think hot vents might reveal clues about the beginnings of life on Earth.

Geysers and More

What happens when you boil water on the stove? Heat from the stove element rises through your kettle and warms the water, right? Within a few minutes, bubbles form and some of the water turns into steam. A dormant volcano can be just like one of the elements on your stove. When magma from Earth's mantle heats underground water, it's time for a splashy show.

Hot Springs

Heated water sometimes seeps through cracks in the crust up to the surface and is trapped in rocky pools called hot springs. For centuries, people have travelled long distances to soak in these natural hot tubs. Many believe that the water of hot springs has special healing properties.

Fumaroles

Fumaroles (steam vents) puff water vapour into the air from cracks in the ground. The hot, moist gases often smell like rotten eggs because they contain the gas sulphur dioxide. When the steam cools, the sulphur condenses, forming yellow crystals around the vent. Changes in fumarole activity sometimes warn that a dormant volcano is about to wake up and erupt again.

Mudpots

Giant mud puddles plop and slurp as hot steam bubbles through them. The mud in these mudpots comes from underground rock that's been dissolved by the acids in the rising steam. Want to take a mud-bath? It's not a great way to get clean, but many people think hot mud is just the thing to soften skin and improve health. Scrub-a-dub mud!

top to bottom: mudpot, hot spring, fumaroles

Geysers

Fountains of hot water and steam shooting high into the air are called geysers. But their performance isn't non-stop. Between spoutings, geysers take breaks that can be as long as several weeks or as short as a few minutes. While most geysers are unpredictable, some spout regularly. For instance, Old Faithful in Yellowstone Park, Wyoming, (pictured right) averages 65 minutes between its spectacular eruptions.

Why do geysers spout, rest and spout again? Because of their underground plumbing. Under a geyser, hot water from deep in the Earth rises into a large hollow, or chamber. When this water boils, bubbles rise and block the narrow pipe to the surface. Pressure builds in the chamber, and the water becomes hotter and hotter. Finally, the bubbles are pushed out, and the super-hot water inside the chamber explodes upward in a spray of water and steam. Whoosh! After each eruption, the geyser takes a break while the chamber refills, then the process begins again.

Putting Nature's Heat to Work

When Vikings discovered Iceland hundreds of years ago, they were amazed to see steam rising from the frozen ground. They named the harbour where they landed Reykjavik, which means "smoking bay." Today, Reykjavik is a busy city. One reason the city has flourished in this cold northern land is its cheap and plentiful source of energy.

Icelanders harness underground steam to turn huge turbines and to produce electricity. They also tap hot groundwater for their businesses and homes. Similar programs are under way in Japan, New Zealand and the United States. This type of energy is called geothermal energy. (*Geothermal* means "Earth's heat.")

Exploring the Earth

Like a team of tiny doctors swarming over a giant-sized patient, scientists are busy probing the Earth. They use symptoms such as earthquakes and volcanoes to figure out what's going on inside the planet today — and what we might see in the future.

New technology helps scientists perform their check-up of Earth. Using special tools, scientists are gaining a better understanding of Earth. Their goal? To make the best use of our planet's resources and to save lives from the destructive forces of earthquakes and volcanoes.

Lasers

By reflecting laser light off mountain tops, scientists can measure even slight changes in the Earth's crust.

Seismographs

Today, seismographs are hooked up to computers to record Earth's trembles and shakes. Because the computers can store and process enormous amounts of data, scientists can analyse and compare hundreds of seismic events.

Satellites

As they orbit the earth, some satellites map our planet and keep watch on remote volcanoes. They beam information to research stations all over the world.

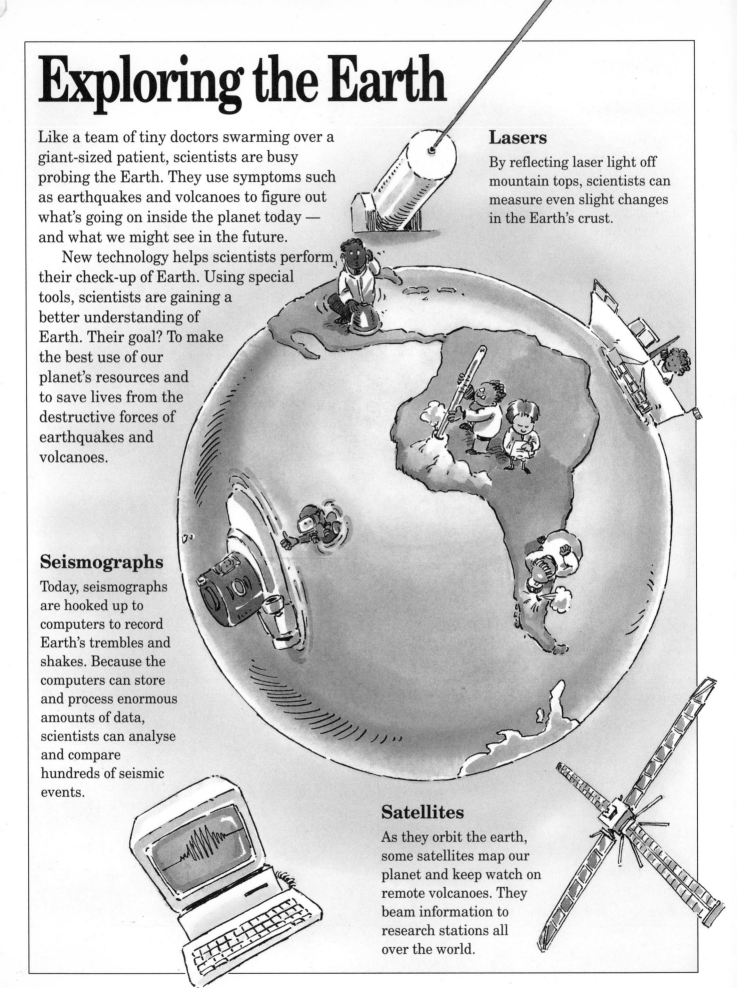

Glossary

core: the centre portion of the Earth

earthquake: a sudden release of energy that shakes the ground

fault: a crack in Earth's crust

geologist: a scientist who studies Earth's crust and interior

geyser: a fountain of hot water and steam that spurts up into the air. The water is heated inside the Earth.

hot spot: a plume of hot liquid rock rising from Earth's mantle

lava: melted rock on Earth's surface

magma: melted rock inside the Earth

mantle: the middle layer of Earth's interior

Pangaea: the ancient supercontinent

rift: a split between tectonic plates

seismologist: a scientist who studies earthquakes

subduction zone: an area where one tectonic plate dives under another

tectonic plates: slabs of Earth's crust and upper mantle layer

volcano: any place where melted rock emerges through the Earth's crust

vulcanologist: a scientist who studies volcanoes

Answers

page 13 If your rolls of toilet paper each have 300 sheets, you would need 15 1/3 rolls to show all of Earth's story.

page 33 It would take 1000 earthquakes of magnitude 4.0 to equal the vibration of one 7.0 quake.

Index

Photo credits

Cover: G.E. Ulrich, Hawaii Volcano Observatory, U.S. Geological Survey (USGS)
page 5: R.E. Wilcox, USGS
page 15: all photos — Department of Natural Resources, State of Washington
page 16–17: D. Wellman, National Oceanic and Atmospheric Administration (NOAA)
page 18: George Walker
page 20: University of Colorado
page 22: top and bottom photos — Joe Nagel; middle photo — J.D. Griggs, Hawaii Volcano Observatory, USGS
page 23: top photo — D. Wellman, NOAA; middle and bottom photos — Joe Nagel
page 24: top photo — G.E. Ulrich, Hawaii Volcano Observatory, USGS; bottom photo — John Latter
page 25: K. Jackson, U.S. Air Force
page 31: National Geophysical Data Centre (NGDC)
page 32: U.S. Department of the Interior
page 37: top photo — NOAA/NGDC; bottom photo — NGDC
page 43: Verena Tunnicliffe
page 44–45: all photos — Joe Nagel